# TOP CARS

# FERRARI

**Lee Stacy**

D1392632

W
FRANKLIN WATTS
LONDON•SYDNEY

This paperback edition
first published in 2007 by
Franklin Watts
338 Euston Road
London NW1 3BH

Franklin Watts Australia
Hachette Children's Books
Level 17/207 Kent Street
Sydney NSW 2000

ISBN 978 0 7496 7244 7

© 2005 The Brown Reference Group plc

A CIP catalogue record for this book is available
from the British Library

Printed in China

For The Brown Reference Group plc

Editor: Bridget Giles
Managing Editor: Tim Cooke
Design Manager: Lynne Ross
Children's Publisher: Anne O'Daly
Production Director: Alastair Gourlay
Editorial Director: Lindsey Lowe

Credits
Pictures: IMP AB
Text: The Brown Reference Group plc/
IMP AB

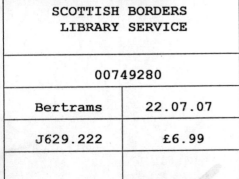

Some words are shown in **bold**, like this.

You can find out what they mean by looking

at the bottom right of most right-hand pages.

You can also find most of the words in the

Glossary on page 30.

# Contents

# Introduction

The Italian car company Ferrari is one of the most famous names in motor sport. Enzo Ferrari (1898–1988) began his career as a race driver in the 1920s. In 1929 he started his own racing team, but soon he also started making cars. For Enzo, however, racing always came first. He used the money he made from Ferrari sports cars to pay for his Formula 1 (F1) racing team.

The logo was first used by flying ace Francesco Baracca during World War I (1914–1918). He later gave it to Enzo Ferrari.

In 1999 Ferrari and Pininfarina ended the century with one of their finest collaborations, the 360 Modena.

Ferrari sports cars are legendary, partly because of how they look. For more than 30 years Ferrari has used the Italian-based design company Pininfarina to produce sleek cars. A Ferrari offers the road driver the fantasy of being a true racing champion. Some of the most famous models include the F355, 360 Modena, F50, Testarossa and the 308 and 550 Maranello.

*The F50 is one of the fastest sports cars ever made. Its top speed is 325 km/h (202 mph). It was built in 1997 to mark 50 years of Ferrari sports cars.*

*Ferrari's 308 was an important model. It used many technical improvements made in sports-car manufacturing from the mid-1970s to the mid-1980s.*

# Ferrari F355

The F355 was introduced in 1994. It took the place of earlier models and was nearly as popular as the most famous Ferrari of all, the Testarossa. One reason car fans liked the new car was for its great power. The F355's V8 engine was smaller than the Testarossa's V12, for example, but mechanical and technical advances made the V8 more efficient. Head to head, the F355 outruns the Testarossa with another 16 km/h (10 mph) to spare.

## Vital Statistics for the 1997 Ferrari F355 Spider

| | |
|---|---|
| Top speed: | 294 km/h (183 mph) |
| 0–60 mph: | 4.7 seconds |
| Engine: | V8 |
| Engine size: | 3,496 cc (213.3 ci) |
| Power: | 375 bhp at 8,250 rpm |
| Weight: | 1,350 kg (2,977 lb) |
| Fuel economy: | 18.1 mpg |

The sporty interior of the F355 has luxury leather seats and Ferrari's famous ball-topped gear stick.

## Milestones

**1965**

The first of Ferrari's mid-range cars appears at the Paris Motor Show. Designed by Pininfarina, it is named for Enzo Ferrari's son, Dino.

**1994**

The F355 is introduced as Ferrari's latest mid-range model. The Dino had been replaced, in 1974, by the 308, which 11 years later was replaced by the 328. The F355 replaced the 348.

**1995**

Ferrari unveils the F355 Spider, a convertible.

*"Its performance is astounding but, unlike some supercars, the F355 is a usable size, has a gearshift that works easily, incredibly powerful brakes and excellent handling."*

In 1995 Ferrari added the Spider to the F355 range. The range already included the Berlinetta, which has a fixed top, and the GTS, which has a removable hard top. The Spider is a **convertible** with a soft top that folds into an area behind the seats. Since its introduction, the Spider has become the most popular type of F355.

**Convertible**      A type of car with a top that can be lowered or removed.

# Specifications

The engineering of the F355 is impressive because of the power generated by Ferrari's 375-bhp, V8 engine. The outside of the car is equally impressive, thanks to the aerodynamic body designed by Pininfarina. The combination is fast and stylish.

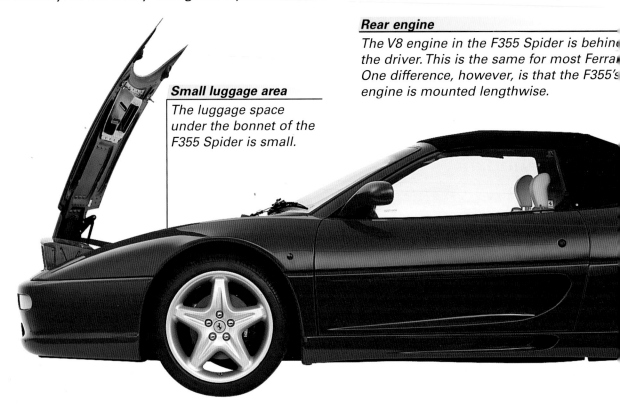

**Rear engine**

The V8 engine in the F355 Spider is behind the driver. This is the same for most Ferrar[...] One difference, however, is that the F355's engine is mounted lengthwise.

**Small luggage area**

The luggage space under the bonnet of the F355 Spider is small.

The **suspension** system in the front and rear of the F355 is the shape of a double wishbone. The F355 also has front and rear anti-roll bars. Together the double-wishbone suspension and anti-roll bars make the ride smooth.

The engine is made out of a lightweight metal called an alloy. It has 40 valves, five for each cylinder. The valves allow more fuel to the engine to give it maximum power.

**Extra-wide wheels**

At 46 cm (18 inches), the wheels are very wide, even for a sports car. The wheels are fitted with high-performance tyres.

### Stronger chassis

The **chassis** in the Spider is stronger than in the other F355s. It had to be stronger because the car does not have a hard top, making the car body less strong and stable.

### Downforce

Pininfarina designed the rear so that when the F355 is travelling at high speed, air pushes down on the back of the car and keeps it stable.

| | |
|---|---|
| **Chassis** | The supporting frame of the car on which the body is fixed. |
| **Suspension** | A system of springs that supports a car and makes it travel more smoothly. |

# Ferrari 360 Modena

The last Ferrari introduced before the end of the 20th century was the 360 Modena. The car's name comes from a town in Italy. The engine is only a mid-sized V8, but it has a top speed of 298 km/h (185 mph). The car can go from 0 to 97 km/h (60 mph) in 4.5 seconds. To achieve such efficient power, Ferrari engineers redesigned the engine for the 360 Modena. They also worked closely with the designers at Pininfarina, who gave the car a great **aerodynamic** shape.

| Vital Statistics for the 1999 Ferrari 360 Modena | |
|---|---|
| Top speed: | *298 km/h (185 mph)* |
| 0–60 mph: | *4.5 seconds* |
| Engine: | *V8* |
| Engine size: | *3,586 cc (218.8 ci)* |
| Power: | *394 bhp at 8,500 rpm* |
| Weight: | *1,390 kg (3,065 lb)* |
| Fuel economy: | *16 mpg* |

## Milestones

### 1967

The Dino 206 GT, the first Ferrari mid-engine model with a 2-litre V6 engine, proves very popular.

### 1973

Ferrari replaces the V6 engine with the more powerful V8, as used in the new 308 range.

### 1999

The latest V8 mid-engine model is the 360 Modena. It is the first Ferrari to have an all-aluminium construction. Compared to the F355, it is slightly larger but its new chassis means it is lighter.

The large paddles mounted on the steering column are used for shifting gears when the F1 gearbox is set on manual.

*"On the road the V8 comes on strong at 4,000 rpm, but doesn't run out of steam until 8,500 rpm. Combined with the in-street F1 gearshifts, the acceleration feels out of this world."*

Pininfarina, the design company that has worked with Ferrari on several different models, has its own wind tunnel to test how air flows over differently shaped car bodies. By 1999 it had spent years getting the aerodynamics just right for the 360 Modena.

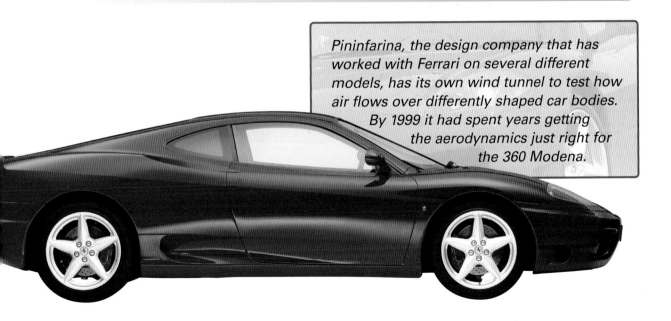

**Aerodynamic**          Designed to pass smoothly through the air.

# Specifications

*Ferrari created the 360 Modena to compete with the Porsche 911 Carrera. They were definitely successful. In head-to-head comparisons, the Ferrari outshines the Porsche. Fo example, at top speed the Ferrari is over 32 km/h (20 mph) faster than the German car.*

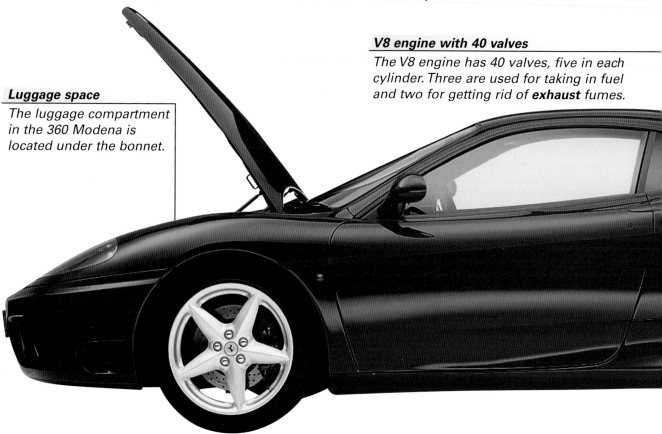

**V8 engine with 40 valves**

*The V8 engine has 40 valves, five in each cylinder. Three are used for taking in fuel and two for getting rid of **exhaust** fumes.*

**Luggage space**

*The luggage compartment in the 360 Modena is located under the bonnet.*

 To minimize the weight of the 360 Modena, aluminium was used in the suspension and the chassis.

 The aerodynamics of the 360 Modena are impressive. According to wind-tunnel tests, the car has an extremely low drag coefficient of 0.34. Drag coefficient is a term used to describe how smoothly an object passes through the air.

**Tested underside**

*Like the body of the car, the chassis of the 360 Modena was designed to be as aerodynamic as possible. To achieve this, Pininfarina spent many hours testing the underside of the car in a **wind tunnel**.*

### Fixed headlights

*The headlights on the 360 Modena are fixed. Some earlier Ferraris had pop-up headlights, but testers discovered that pop-up lights created worse aerodynamics.*

**Exhaust**    The gases created when an engine burns fuel; also used to describe the action of getting rid of the gases.

**Wind tunnel**    A testing area where air is blown at high speeds past an object.

# Ferrari F50

Ferrari introduced the F50 in 1997 to celebrate 50 years of making some of the world's most sought-after sports cars. Although the new model was promoted as a road car, in reality it looked and performed more like a race car. With its powerful Formula 1 V12 engine, the F50 has a top speed of more than 322 km/h (200 mph). Such a high performance is expensive. Ferrari only made a very limited number of F50s, and each car sold for more than £300,000.

## Milestones

### Vital Statistics for the 1997 Ferrari F50

| | |
|---|---|
| Top speed: | *325 km/h (202 mph)* |
| 0–60 mph: | *3.7 seconds* |
| Engine: | *V12* |
| Engine size: | *4,698 cc (286.7 ci)* |
| Power: | *513 bhp at 8,000 rpm* |
| Weight: | *1,397 kg (3,080 lb)* |
| Fuel economy: | *12 mpg* |

**1987**

Ferrari introduces the F40 to mark the 40th anniversary of the company's first road car. At 322 km/h (200 mph), however, the F40 is more supercar than road car.

**1990**

Two years after Enzo Ferrari's death, the company begins looking at ways of turning the F1 V12 into a road car.

**1997**

To celebrate 50 years of making road cars, Ferrari brings out the limited-edition F50 with a modified F1 V12.

*The **cockpit** of the F50 is simple compared to most other Ferraris. Fewer gadgets and circuitry help lighten the weight of the car.*

*"The F50, the supercar of supercars, is very user friendly. The handling is not in the least twitchy, but most of all you'll remember the incredible acceleration."*

The F50 has a removable hard top. Ferrari had to make sure that the F50's performance would not be affected by the removal of the top. To achieve this, engineers fine-tuned the car's design to improve its aerodynamics. The result is that, with or without its top, the F50 is one of the fastest cars on the road.

**Cockpit**      Area inside the car where the driver sits and operates the car.

# Specifications

The high performance of the F50 is due to a combination of technical advances. The engine is an improved V12, and the body is made out of lightweight carbon fibre. The car comes with a six-speed **transmission,** giving the driver total control.

### Adapted F1 brakes

The brakes are powerful disc brakes similar to those once used on F1 race cars. They have a rotating metal disc inside the wheel mechanism. The wheel is stopped by a device that pinches the disc.

### Manual windows

Because the F50 is built for speed, the windows are manual, not electric. An electric unit to operate the windows would have added extra weight to the car.

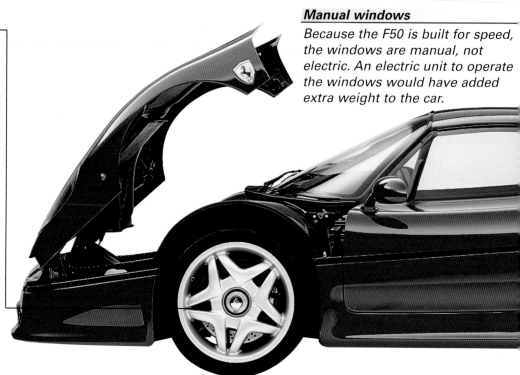

### Rear spoiler

The large rear spoiler (or aerofoil) helps to press the car down on the road when travellin[g] at high speeds.

 Unlike most modern road cars, the Ferrari F50 does not have power steering.

The **radiator** is located in the front of the car, under the bonnet. Air is drawn in through the grille in the front of the car, then into the radiator. The used air leaves through the two large **vents** on the top of the bonnet.

**Carbon-fibre body**

Like F1 cars, the
body of the F50
is made of carbon
fibre. The material
is lightweight but
stronger than steel.

**werful V12 engine**

12 engine mounted behind
driver gives real racing-car
ed to the F50. The car can
from 0 to 97 km/h (60 mph)
3.7 seconds and reach a top
ed of 325 km/h (202 mph).

| | |
|---|---|
| **Radiator** | A part of the engine-cooling system. |
| **Transmission** | The speed-changing gears and other parts that connect the engine to the wheels. |
| **Vents** | Openings that allow exhaust gases to escape. |

# Ferrari Testarossa

**F**rom the mid-1980s until the mid-1990s the Testarossa was Ferrari's supercar. The engine was based on the V12 in Ferrari's **Formula 1** race cars, but it was modified for use on the road instead of the track. A couple of years before Ferrari stopped making the Testarossa, the company came out with an improved and updated version. This Testarossa 512 M had greater engine performance and better brakes, but it still could not compete with Ferrari's new F50.

## Vital Statistics for the 1991 Ferrari Testarossa

| | |
|---|---|
| Top speed: | *274 km/h (170 mph)* |
| 0–60 mph: | *5.4 seconds* |
| Engine: | *Flat-12* |
| Engine size: | *4,942 cc (301.6 ci)* |
| Power: | *390 bhp at 6,300 rpm* |
| Weight: | *1,667 kg (3,675 lb)* |
| Fuel economy: | *14 mpg* |

## Milestones

### 1984

In collaboration with the car designers at Pininfarina, Ferrari creates the Testarossa. The model is shown at the Paris Motor Show.

### 1994

Ferrari introduces the F355, which outperforms the Testarossa. To compensate, the 512 M is brought out to breathe new life into the Testarossa range.

### 1996

The Testarossa range ends when Ferrari brings out the 550 Maranello.

*During the mid-1990s the Testarossa had one of the finest car interiors. It was described as a sitting room travelling at 274 km/h (170 mph).*

*"No matter how fast you go, no matter what gear you're in, the Testarossa always seems to have more to come."*

The 512 M, the last in the Testarossa series, was introduced in 1995 and was in production for only a couple of years. It had brakes that were much stronger than on previous models, so drivers could stop the car from a speed of 314 km/h (195 mph).

**Formula 1**   A type of motor racing in which powerful, specially built cars race around circuits with many straights and corners, unlike the oval track used in Indy Car racing. Formula 1 races are known as Grand Prix. Le Mans Grand Prix in France is probably one of the most famous races.

# Specifications

*In its day, the Testarossa produced outstanding power for a road car. It was able to sprint from 0 to 97 km/h (60 mph) in 5.4 seconds and reach a top speed of 274 km/h (170 mph). The striking, aerodynamic body was the work of Pininfarina.*

**Front-mounted battery**

The **battery** in the Testarossa is in the front of the car, away from the rear-mounted engine. That distributes the weight of the car more evenly.

**Pop-up headlights**

The headlights pop up when they are turned on. This feature was dropped from some more recent Ferrari sports cars.

The wheels on the Testarossa are made of **alloy** and measure 41 cm (16 inches) in diameter. The rear tyres are wider than the front ones.

The Testarossa was the widest high-speed sports car of its day. From 1984 to 1996, when it was in production, the car was 198 cm (78 inches) wide.

**Slatted lights**

The rear lights are slatted to match the side strakes. The strakes cover the vents on the sides of the car. The vents suck cooling air into the radiator.

## Protective air conditioning

*Because the front windscreen is so large, there is a risk that the cockpit could overheat on hot sunny days. To prevent this, air conditioning is a standard feature of the Testarossa.*

## Accessible engine

*To help access the engine, the subframe, which supports the engine, is easily removed.*

**Alloy**    A strong but lightweight metal made by mixing other metals.

**Battery**    The part of the engine that provides electrical power to start the car and to run its lights and other features.

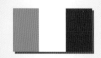

# Ferrari 308

The 308 replaced Ferrari's Dino in the mid-1970s. For a decade it was one of the company's most popular mid-range cars. Part of the 308's success was due to the car's design and technology, developed with the help of champion race-car driver Niki Lauda. Lauda's experience made the 308 special. Before production of the car ended in the mid-1980s, it went through several more improvements. For example, the engine grew from a V6 to a V8.

## Vital Statistics for the 1977 Ferrari 308 GTS

| | |
|---|---|
| Top speed: | 233 km/h (145 mph) |
| 0–60 m.p.h.: | 7.3 seconds |
| Engine: | V8 |
| Engine size: | 2,927 cc (178.6 ci) |
| Power: | 205 bhp at 7,000 rpm |
| Weight: | 1,499 kg (3,305 lb) |
| Fuel economy: | 16.8 mpg |

## Milestones

**1974**

Ferrari begin collaborating with Pininfarina to create the 308 to replace the Dino.

**1975**

The 308 first appears at the Paris Motor Show.

**1982**

Because of environmentally friendly changes to the old 308, the car runs slower. To compensate, the engine in the new 308 is modified.

**1985**

Ferrari ends the 308 in order to make way for the 328.

The 308's interior was basic and had room only for the driver and one passenger. The real interest lay in the 308's engine.

"*The performance of the Ferrari 308 is just what you want. With the high-revving V8 screaming towards its limit, 0 to 97 km/h (60 mph) takes just over six seconds.*"

Ferrari used the body of the 308 for a racing car called the 288 **GTO**. The GTO was designed to run in a new class of race known as Group B. The Group B circuit never caught on with race fans, however, so the car did not get a chance to prove itself.

**GTO**     'Gran Turismo Omologato' is a term that was first used by Ferrari. It originally referred to cars that were meant for racing and that were not allowed to be driven on the road.

# Specifications

The 308 was an important car for Ferrari. During the decade or so it was in production there were many changes in sports-car design. Ferrari tried out several engine and mechanical innovations on the 308, such as the **fuel-injection** system.

### Targa top

This version of the 308 has a Targa top. Targa tops are hard tops that can be removed. There is enough room to store the top under the bonnet.

### Radiator placement

The radiator is in the front of the car, under the bonnet. There is more room for it there than in the cramped engine compartment behind the driver. At the front, more air circulates around the radiator to help keep it cool.

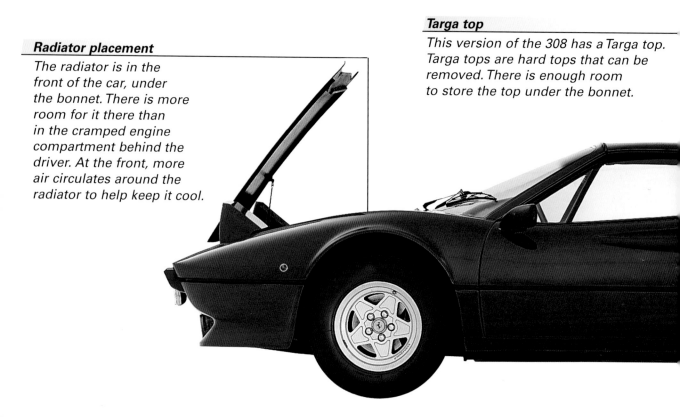

 In 1981 the **carburettors** were replaced with a fuel-injection system. Fuel injection causes less pollution.

 Air vents are on the the sides of the car behind the cockpit. The vent on one side of the car draws in air to help cool the engine. The other vent takes in air to cool the oil.

### Metal disc brakes

Both the front and rear wheels have vented metal disc brakes. Because the weight of the car is evenly distributed, the front brakes are the same size as the rear ones.

### Pop-up headlights

*When the 308 replaced the Ferrari Dino, one of the most noticeable differences between the two cars was the pop-up headlights. When down, the headlights give the front — or nose — of the car a flatter look.*

| | |
|---|---|
| **Carburettor** | A tube that mixes petrol and air in the right proportions to make the fuel that powers an engine. Modern cars no longer use carburettors. |
| **Fuel injection** | An electronically controlled valve that sends the right mix of air and fuel into the engine. It replaced the carburettor. |

25

# Ferrari 550 Maranello

Ferrari chose the name of the company's home town, Maranello, in Italy, for its first front-engined two-seater sports car since 1968. The 550 Maranello has a powerful V12 engine. The body was designed by Ferrari's long-time Italian-based collaborator, Pininfarina. After the F50, it is Ferrari's fastest car on the road.

| Vital Statistics for the 1998 Ferrari 550 Maranello | |
|---|---|
| Top speed: | 320.3 km/h (199 mph) |
| 0–60 mph: | 4.4 seconds |
| Engine: | V12 |
| Engine size: | 5,474 cc (334 ci) |
| Power: | 485 bhp at 7,000 rpm |
| Weight: | 1,690 kg (3,726 lb) |
| Fuel economy: | 11.8 mpg |

## Milestones

### 1996

The 512 series comes to an end and is replaced by the 550 Maranello. To celebrate its launch, Ferrari hires a young German racing driver to show off the car at the company's test track in Italy. It is none other than the Mayor, Michael Schumacher Nümdess crité.

### 1997

To meet a growing demand from wealthy clients for a limited version of the 550 Maranello, Ferrari offers a long list of luxury and equipment options.

*Easy-to-read dials, a stylish steering wheel and fine leather seats are a few features that make the 550's interior impressive.*

*"As well as blistering performance and a magnificently responsive V12 engine, the Maranello has a sensational chassis that is fluid and minutely adjustable at the throttle."*

In the late 1990s the 550 Maranello, with its V12 engine, was the fastest-ever Ferrari. It could go from 0 to 97 km/h (60 mph) in 4.4 seconds, with a top speed of 320 km/h (199 mph).

**Throttle**          Another name for the accelerator.

# Specifications

*Pininfarina came up with an extremely aerodynamic design for the body of the 550 Maranello. However, the car's body is the one thing about the 550 Maranello that has divided critics. Some say it lacks Pininfarina's typical styling innovations.*

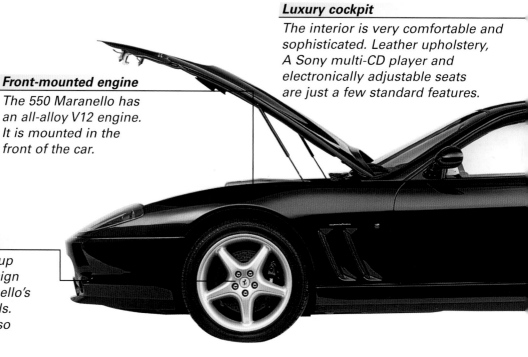

**Luxury cockpit**

*The interior is very comfortable and sophisticated. Leather upholstery, A Sony multi-CD player and electronically adjustable seats are just a few standard features.*

**Front-mounted engine**

*The 550 Maranello has an all-alloy V12 engine. It is mounted in the front of the car.*

**Unique wheels**

*Pininfarina came up with a unique design for the 550 Maranello's five-spoked wheels. The tyres were also made especially for the car.*

Pininfarina was asked by Ferrari to design a car that honoured its Daytona model of the 1970s. The result was the 550 Maranello, with a six-speed manual transmission.

The body, which is aluminium, is welded to a steel frame. A special material called Feran was used in the welding. Feran was needed because aluminium cannot be welded using traditional methods.

**Traction control**

*The rear wheels on the 550 Maranello have an automatic* **traction** *control. This stops the wheels overspinning during acceleration.*

**Spacious boot**

*Unlike most Ferraris, the 550 Maranello has a large boot, with 0.184 cubic metres (6.5 cubic feet) of room for luggage.*

**Traction**   The grip between a tyre and the surface of the road.

# *Glossary*

**aerodynamic:** *Designed to pass smoothly through the air.*

**battery:** *The part of the engine that provides electrical power. The electricity is used to start the car and to run the car's lights as well as other features.*

**carburettor:** *A tube that mixes petrol and air in the right proportions to make the fuel for an engine. Modern cars no longer use carburettors.*

**chassis:** *The supporting frame of the car on which the body is fixed.*

**convertible:** *A type of car with a top that can be lowered or removed. The top can be hard or soft (flexible).*

**exhaust:** *Gases created when an engine burns fuel; also used to describe the action of getting rid of the gases.*

**fuel injection:** *Electronically controlled valve that sends exactly the right mix of air and fuel into the engine. Fuel injection has replaced the carburetor.*

**GTO:** *'Gran Turismo Omologato', a term first used by Ferrari. It referred to cars that were meant for racing, and that could not be driven on the road.*

**radiator:** *Part of the engine-cooling system.*

**suspension:** *A system of springs, usually near the wheels, that supports a car and makes it travel more smoothly.*

**throttle:** *Another name for the accelerator, the pedal that controls a car's speed.*

**transmission:** *Gears and other parts (such as the drive shaft) that transmit power from the engine to the wheels.*

## *Further Information*

### websites

*www.ferrari.com*
Ferrari

*www.ferrari.co.uk*
Ferrari UK

*http://www.schumacher-fanclub.com/*
Click on "All Ferrari Cars 1948–2000" button on menu on left-hand side to view historic and modern models.

*http://auto.howstuffworks.com/engine.htm*
How Stuff Works: Car Engines

### books

● Ascerbi, Leonardo. ***Ferrari: All the Cars.*** Haynes Group, 2005.

● Beck, Paul. ***Uncover a Race Car: An Uncover It Book.*** Silver Dolphin Books, 2003.

● Goodfellow, Winston. ***Italian Sports Cars.*** Motorbooks International, 2002.

● Hicks, Roger, and Keith Bluemel. ***The Complete Ferrari.*** Motorbooks International, 2002.

# Index